Finding Peace
in the
Promise

*A Memoir
of Walking with Intention*

Aubrie Abernethy

*For my dear friend,
Frances* ♡

Enjoy the Journey

Aubrie Abernethy

Finding Peace in the Promise
A Memoir of Walking with Intention
Aubrie Abernethy

Published October 2024
Little Creek Books
Imprint of Jan-Carol Publishing, Inc
All rights reserved
Copyright © 2024 by Aubrie Abernethy

This book may not be reproduced in whole or part, in any matter whatsoever without written permission, with the exception of brief quotations within book reviews or articles.

ISBN: 978-1-962561-50-1
Library of Congress Control Number: 2024947944

You may contact the publisher:
Jan-Carol Publishing, Inc
PO Box 701
Johnson City, TN 37605
publisher@jancarolpublishing.com
www.jancarolpublishing.com

*To any walker who may read this book
and become inspired to make a promise to themselves…
step out, one foot at a time, and walk.
Believe you can, and you will!
Many insights await you!*

Foreword

By Pam Blair
Author, *Life is Precious: Lessons in Healthy Living,
Surviving Cancer, and Recovering from Grief* (Chapel Hill Press)

I met Aubrie Abernethy more than 12 years ago when I became a member of the Mountain View Garden Club, where Aubrie has served for 35 years. I was warmly welcomed by her and was immediately impressed with her energy and vitality, especially when we served as program co-chairs of the club for two consecutive years. With Aubrie's diverse interests and numerous contacts in the community, planning programs with her was a joyful learning experience.

When Aubrie told me of her plan to walk 1,000 miles to mark her 75th birthday, I had no doubt that she would reach her goal. But walking 1,000 miles was not all that she accomplished; she found a way to log her miles virtually to help organizations in need. This is not surprising, because when Aubrie makes a commitment, she invests herself totally and always goes above and beyond. She was a founding member, volunteer, and on the board of directors at One Acre Café, a nonprofit café in Johnson City that served the food-insecure for more than 10 years. Her love and knowledge of butterflies, birds, and Roan Mountain are documented in newspaper articles and other publications, and her passion as a former teacher and tutor has touched the lives of countless young people and future leaders.

Aubrie has a special gift for writing so descriptively that you will feel like you are walking with her as she logs the miles on her journey. With many interesting locations, informative sidebars, and funny conversations with family members who occasionally joined her, you will wish you could have tagged along. Achieving the goal of walking 1,000 miles is not the end of her journey, but the beginning of something even greater. I can't wait to see what lies ahead for her.

Prologue

This book is a story about a visualization I had as a milestone in my life was approaching. After deeply reflecting on the 75 years I had traveled on planet Earth, I envisioned myself as a healthier and less anxious person who would be able to become more fully engaged in life with my family and friends. I needed to become more conscious of "doing" less and "being" more... being more of what matters most.

I sought peace and contentment. I made a promise to myself as I contemplated a way of celebrating my 75th trip around the sun. An active experience is what I sought, one that would mark the year with gratitude for the genetics I had inherited and the good fortune of a generally healthy life. Length is one thing, but quality of life is another. I wanted to be proactive in creating a way to move forward into the last 25 years of my century, living as health conscious as I had been most of my first 75 years. Now, I'd be kidding myself if I said there had not been distractions to healthy living, especially making healthy food and drink choices. Throughout my life, the greatest temptations that drew me in were sugar and adult beverages. I still have a love-hate relationship with sugar, especially chocolate. I do love that creamy, rich texture and the feel-good effects of dark chocolate. I associate it with pure joy! My relationship with alcohol, however, was noxious. I believed it could relieve my anxiety and that sense of confoundedness I experienced within. Relief using alcohol was a false presumption. I took a close look at myself and made a conscious choice to stop consuming a substance that was stealing my creativity, vitality, and quality of life. That was New Year's Eve, 2017. My quandary became choosing a path to blaze in search of achieving anxiety relief and balancing my sweet tooth.

Figuring the next 25 years would include my "sunset" years, a time to reflect and live life more intentionally, I chose a path I believed could sustain me for the long haul. No "pie in the sky" quick fixes for me. I was thoughtful about my strengths that could help me in my decision-making. As I pondered what that might be, I realized my greatest nemesis in my teenage years and young womanhood might be the key. At times, I cursed my familial trait of having heavy legs, the mighty oaks with hefty trunks. Back then, they were a source of embarrassment when "thin" was in and I was not...thin. As the years passed, I began to realize my legs had always served me well. I played basketball as a guard and was voted most valuable player. I loved hiking trails wherever I traveled, both near and far away. I loved chasing my two very active and athletic daughters and enthusiastically serving the communities in which I lived, all with feet on the ground. Realizing those strong legs were on my side as an asset, not an embarrassment, it became clear that those legs were made for walking! *I promised myself I would intentionally walk 1,000 miles by year's end.*

I began walking on January 1, 2022. The mantra I had read that most clearly expressed my feelings and purpose was, "She believed she could, so she did." That was it! I adopted this mantra, and the journey began.

Walking became the way of bringing clarity to my life and continues to excite me into the next 25 years' adventures and goals of good health.

Family and friends followed me as I journeyed those miles, asking, "How's your walking challenge going? How many more miles do you have to go? How do you stay motivated? You're an inspiration! I'm only half your age, and I couldn't do it." My empathetic response was, "Sure you can!" Once again, I shared the mantra I had adopted: "She believed she could, so she did."

Belief in one's ability to do something is fine and good, but what else was there? I *needed to do* this for my own health as I pursued relief from the anxiety I experienced. I also *needed to do* this to stay strong for those around me whom I love. During life's difficult times, I *wanted to be* fully present, strong in mind and body. I am human and fall short sometimes, but my hope was that by staying physically strong, I would better be able to cope mentally with adventures on the horizon. So, I walked.

Chapter 1

LOCATIONS

There were six locations that my heart and "soles" considered, as soil, sand, and rocky paths called my name for walking those 1,000 miles. These places and I have history and important memories that helped to shape my life. The six locations included my home territory, Althea Street, and its surrounding neighborhood, Johnson City, TN; the home of my oldest grandson, Atlanta, GA; the home of my youngest grandson, Apex, NC; a place of deep connection, Roan Mountain, TN; a place of family beach outings for over 80 years, Pawleys Island/Litchfield Beach, SC; and my husband's and my winter retreat, Hermosa Beach, Costa Rica.

A seventh location, and my fallback during inclement weather, was The Mall at Johnson City, TN.

MY HOME TERRITORY

My home territory encompassed the streets surrounding Althea Street, a quiet street with families homesteading there for many years, and an area I knew best. While topographically, Althea Street itself is relatively flat, there is one significant hill rising on an adjacent street. It was the road most traveled. When the weather was foreboding, I could stay close to home. Should I need to make a run for it, I could get back home quickly. Other times, this close-to-home walk just felt familiar and comfortable. My observations of sights and sounds around me were keen.

Just down the street, I passed a little stone cottage with green wood siding that seemed uninhabited. Occasionally, a trash can was moved, or there was a rare sighting of a vehicle parked in front of the charming yet mysterious cottage. The curtains were always closed, but the grass and weeds were mowed from time to time. One day, I walked past the large field that adjoined the little stone cottage. I observed a middle-aged man near an old farm truck laden with limbs and brush of all sizes. I stopped and called to him, saying, "That looks like a lot of work on such a beautiful day." He stopped what he was doing and walked over to me. He introduced himself and began to explain that he was clearing out some dead wood for the city to pick up on their next run through the neighborhood.

We chatted a bit about our neighbors and the neighborhood in general. I asked him if he knew who owned the little stone cottage, and to my astonishment, he replied that he did! The conversation that ensued between two new friends revealed that he had owned it for many years, but he didn't live in it. This explained my observations of vacancy. He said, at one time, he considered fixing it up for occupancy, but never did live in it. He used it occasionally when he needed a quiet place to do his work or think but was considering selling it. I asked him if I might take a look inside, and he cordially responded, "Of course!" It was charming in every sense of the word. Walls and ceilings were constructed of wormy chestnut, floors were a type of maple, and the stone fireplace and roughhewn mantle created an image of a cozy evening, lively conversations, listening to music, or sinking into a comfy chair while getting lost in a good book. You could almost take in the aromas of the quaint nearby kitchen. Its pots and pans neatly hung on hooks, and hand-painted ceramic plates with beautiful floral designs graced the open cabinets. Windows facing the fields in back of the cottage promised bucolic scenes of rabbits hopping hither and yon, birds creating symphonic renditions, and children joyfully playing hide-and-go-seek, kick-the-can, or lazily stargazing in the expanse of newly mown grass. Learning that the cottage was built in 1932, I began imagining the times past, of supper conversations and life in this bygone era. The two bedrooms were warm and inviting, promising nostalgic dreams from another time. I was transfixed and could have stayed longer. I told the owner of my walks that I had passed by frequently, imagining the stories the little cottage could tell. He laughed and replied, "Oh, there are many!" Serendipitous encounters, such as this one, arose from time to time, enriching the human experiences of walking.

There was another chance encounter as Molly, our small dog, and I headed out to walk one sunny spring day. Molly eagerly pulled forward with enthusiasm as my upper body strained against the tug of her leash. Who knew 13 pounds of dog could be so strong and insistent?

Our walking eventually settled into a *sniff-stop-walk, sniff-stop-walk* pattern as we made our way around the neighborhood. On the corner of our street, a new young couple, whom I had not met, had moved in. As we passed by, Molly immediately began wagging her tail with great joy as she spotted a young child trying to walk. We slowly approached the young mother and her child, introducing ourselves to them. The young child was the focus of our attention, and Molly was the focus of the child's attention! They became fast friends as squeals from the child filled the air and "kisses" from Molly were slathered on the child.

What I noticed was not only the joy being displayed by the two new friends, but also the motivation of the child to walk toward Molly. The child toddled unsteadily and reached Molly with a plop to the ground, anticipating more kisses! The motivation to walk is an individual choice, whether it is to greet another person (or animal), or freely put one foot in front of the other and see where it leads you. Sometimes, it is good to be reminded to keep your eye on the goal, just as the young child had done.

A wave is defined as a movement with your hand to signify a feeling or emotion. In times past, porch-sitting went hand in hand with neighbors greeting one another with a wave to say, "Hello." As I walked, waving became part of my ritual. Frequently, I waved as neighbors mowed their lawns, planted flowers, repaired their houses, or actually porch-sat. The return wave was a sign of recognition between neighbors; that feeling of, "We're in it together," during this time of our lives.

There's also the caring wave that goes mostly unseen. As each season moved to the next, "life" happened in the neighborhood. There were births, deaths, serious illness, and loneliness, as well as those times of contentment. As I became aware of these life events occurring inside the homes of others, I began gently waving in the direction of specific houses. Sometimes I'd pause for a minute, directing positive energy toward my neighbor's home. Then, I'd resume walking, one foot in front of the other. Later on, some neighbors remarked, saying that they had seen me waving, and it had brightened their day. It's the small things that count.

Spring is my favorite season for walking. All of nature awakens, and the sounds, sights, and smells are intoxicating. Birds are twitterpated as they sing echoing songs from pre-dawn to post-twilight. Their melodies are deafening at times, but music to my ears as I walked. Birds' springtime exuberance indicates the availability of abundant nesting and feeding habitat throughout the neighborhood. Slowing my walking pace, I drank it all in—the sights of delicate dogwood blooms opening, squirrels scampering and leaping from tree to tree as if their race would never end. Baby bunnies innocently emerged from the thicket to munch on fresh clover, while bluebirds flashed their colorful feathers as they fluttered about examining the bird box as a potential nesting site for perhaps five eggs. Their paired behavior showed one standing guard atop the house, while the other checked out the suitability of the interior. From afar, I visually monitored the activities in neighborhood boxes as I walked past. Seeing the fledglings attempt their first flight gave me a sense of pure joy. My hope was that some would return to raise a brood of their own as they followed their territorial instinct of returning to their birth territory.

The most aromatic fragrance along my spring walks was the fringe tree in my neighbor's yard. The fringe tree gets its name from its clouds of fleecy white, soft, fragrant flowers that hang from branches in late spring. As I approached this beautiful tree, I slowed down, closed my eyes, and lost myself for a moment as its bouquet swept into my consciousness and transported me to a euphoric place. Oh, the splendor of springtime walking, one foot in front of the other. *Sigh.*

Chapter 2

MY GRANDSONS' TERRITORIES: ATLANTA, GA AND APEX, NC

Two other neighborhoods were a delightful part of my walking challenge. These were the neighborhoods of my grandsons, one in Atlanta, the other in Apex. The seven-year age difference between the boys determined the "style" of walking we enjoyed together. When you're 10 years old, you're more interested in walking *to a place*, like the local froyo shop a few blocks from home. While walking, we'd chat about our preferred flavors, any toppings we might choose, and whether we'd sit inside or outside. My grandson's top choices for flavors of froyo included orange meringue, cheesecake, and vanilla in a cup with plenty of room for an abundance of delicious toppings. Seeing all the colorful toppings spread out in the display made our mouths water; so many choices. My grandson narrowed it down to gummy bears, Swedish fish, gummy worms, sprinkles, and the little round red balls that oozed cherry or strawberry liquid. My preferences always included chocolate brownie bites and various combos of decadent froyo flavors of chocolate mania, peanut butter, key lime pie, or raza-ma-taz!

Whatever concoctions we created tasted heavenly, and our conversations were interrupted with interjections of, "Yum! Ooooooo, I love when one squirts on the inside of my cheek! Ohhh, this is de-li-cious! *Slurp*, this is amazing!" Our sweet tooth completely satisfied, the walk back home was more of an amble. Our pace slowed, and the conversations turned to our favorite art projects, Michigan football, and girls. I'm not sure who enjoyed it most.

There was another place my 10-year-old grandson enjoyed in Atlanta. Our walking conversations to the neighborhood Variety Store revolved around what small treasures we might find there. You never knew what might be tucked in the back of a shelf, so we had to search, sometimes for an hour or so, until the treasure of treasures said, "Take me home!" High on the list of found treasures were old school toys like mini buggies, cap guns, pocket watches, and a small music box that played Beethoven. Now, that was a hard choice!

A walk to the Variety Store would not be complete without exploring the candy aisle. It was not the usual candy you'd find at the grocery store. Instead, there were cool things like gummy sushi, gummy pizza, and Dip-N-Stix. The winner-takes-all candy was named Beanboozled. These were meant to be gourmet jellybeans. Now, that was a real stretch, because if you chose brown ones, they would taste like chocolate or dog food! I don't know about you, but my grandson and I are not fond of eating dog food. Wasn't that made for dogs, as the name indicated? Then, there were the blue ones that tasted like blueberry or toothpaste. That one was tolerable, but stay away from the multicolored ones unless you are willing to risk tutti frutti or stinky socks!

Those were special times spent together on a simple walk. Connecting by walking and talking had a way of deepening our relationship. All we needed to do was put one foot in front of the other and start talking as we enjoyed the spontaneity of the present moment.

The "style" of walking with a 3-year-old is always an adventure, not a predetermined direction. While I suggested a starting direction by saying, "Let's go this way," my grandson often had a different idea, and he usually won! So, we headed out frequently with his wheelbarrow in tow. We searched the sidewalk areas for sticks and other treasures of nature. An area where pinecones and pine needles were abundant drew his attention. He loaded his wheelbarrow, scoops at a time, delighting in the process. Ideas of how to use the pinecones and pine needles popped into his imagination. He chattered away! Many times, we walked down the hill with a load of woodsy treasures.

When we arrived back at the pine trees alongside the sidewalk, he returned the cones and needles back to nature. They would still be there for another day's trek up the hill. Repetition of this walk the next day brought familiar fun and chatter, or we chose a new adventure...with binoculars!

Kid-friendly binoculars can open a child's imagination like no other toy. Three-year-olds, like my grandson, are wide-eyed and curious, often taking in large expanses around them. There is no better way to sharpen the focus on a unique aspect of Mother Nature that catches the attention of a child than using binoculars. The boys next door gave my grandson a pair of binoculars that oftentimes were part of the gear he carried along with us. A child who wears binoculars around his neck walks with anticipation and purpose. All of nature pops out, like weeds in the cracks in the sidewalk, cardinals, trees, chickadees, dandelions, bugs, squirrel's nests, and oh, so many other wonders of the neighborhood we explored.

In today's world, so many children are missing out on the free and easily accessible areas in their own backyards and neighborhoods where adventures await. I believe we, as parents, grandparents, and family, have a responsibility to encourage the simple pleasures of a walk with a child and share the sights, sounds, and smells all around us. Nature is resilient in spite of humans' bad choices. However, the next generation needs information about the challenges that will face them. They also need nurturing conversations about the importance of being keenly aware of their impact on future generations. It is incumbent upon us to begin guiding our young children and teens toward knowledge and practice in their daily lives. Consider walking with a young person somewhere, anywhere, and engaging them in this important matter. You might be surprised at the conversation that ensues and the difference it may make in that wonderful life.

During our walks, my grandsons and I bonded and made memories together, hopefully ones that would sustain them as they mature. While I was known by them as Gigi, they will always be "my boys." Our walks were like no other.

Chapter 3

ROAN MOUNTAIN:
THE CROWN JEWEL OF THE APPALACHIANS

My walks extended vertically from sea level to 6,285 feet at Roan High Bluff on Roan Mountain. The history of this mountain and my family's connection to it inspired me to explore on foot just as generations before me did. The first foot travelers to Roan Mountain were Native Americans who lived at the base of the mountains and traveled across the gaps. In the late 18th Century, the first botanists who explored this glorious stretch of dense fir and spruce forests, grassy ridges, balds, and mountain peaks were André Michaux, John Fraser, and Asa Gray. They studied and documented many rare plant communities, including the Catawba rhododendron, the Fraser fir, and Grays lily. Many foot travelers were emboldened to follow them...including me.

The writings of John Muir, premier botanist and environmental activist, indicate that during 1898, he explored Roan Mountain and described his experiences amidst this unique wilderness with its diverse plants, many of which were new to the world. The realization that my maternal grandmother, having been born in 1882, was alive and camping on Roan Mountain during these times was astonishing to me. In my teenage years, my grandmother, lovingly known by me as "Granny," told me about times she and her friends, male and female, made the day-long trek by hack, a horse-drawn buggy, to Roan Mountain, where they set up camp overnight by a cool mountain stream.

John Muir

My grandparents far left, top row

She described the difficulty of this for women especially, since their attire consisted of pantaloons and long skirts pulled in snugly around the waist, long sleeved and to-the-neck blouses, leather shoes, and stockings. A hat, of course, topped off the outfit. These outings of my grandmother and her friends occurred at the same time John Muir was collecting specimens and hiking on Roan Mountain. I wonder if their paths ever crossed!

My parents were dating in the mid-1930s and often drove the trek from Johnson City to special spots along the overlooks on Roan Mountain, where they met friends for walks and picnics. Some years later, my father was hired to design the cabins in the area that is now in Roan Mountain State Park. They were nestled into the forest in such a manner that the fewest trees would need to be cut. Over the years, hundreds of adventurers made those cabins the base from which they explored the many trails and places of wonder.

As an adult, I was drawn back to Roan Mountain, where walks and hikes stirred something in me, just as it had for my grandparents' and parents' generations before. Spending weekends with friends in the cabins seemed like home to me. As my head melted into the pillow at night, a sense of peaceful rest swept over me—oh, beautiful sleep. As the new day dawned, my senses came alive again, and I was transported to a different time when all of this was untouched wilderness, and I imagined myself there...then.

These experiences, recollected from my family or lived by me, all occurred because I began to walk the trails my family had

Painting of Roan Mountain by the author.

walked years before. Those walks and hikes continue to this day and reawaken a feeling of being fully alive with each step, deeply rooted to the place called Roan Mountain. So, you see, the love I feel for walking the trails of Roan Mountain is in my DNA.

Chapter 4

BEACHSIDE LOCATIONS

My walking challenge took place in several beachside locations spanning both the Atlantic and Pacific Oceans. For several winters, my husband and I traveled to Hermosa Beach, Costa Rica, for an extended stay. This black volcanic beach was located 45 minutes north of Manuel Antonio National Park and was off the beaten path. Bungalow #8, only steps away from the Pacific Ocean, became home. There was a diversity of people who were renters, as we were, and others who owned their piece of paradise. Twenty-six bungalows ("beach houses") were situated in a horseshoe layout and were staggered for optimum views. There was a pool and community ranchero. Quite a lucky find for us. We had no car and walked into the surfing village for supplies or caught a ride into nearby Jaco for weekly groceries. The temperature was tropical, and most days were gloriously sunny and perfect for daily beach walks alongside the glimmering water and crashing waves enticing eager surfers to catch a wave. The sights and sounds of the rhythmic ocean waves became a balm to my city-stressed soul.

I loved those peaceful walks with my hair blowing in the gentle sea breezes and my skin soaking in the warmth of the equatorial sun. The volcanic black sand prevented most barefoot walking, so I donned my comfy rainbow tie-dyed walking shoes and strode four to five miles per day. Sometimes, the ocean waves set the cadence for my walking. Other times, I listened to an audiobook as the rhythm of my body moved me smoothly down the line of palms along the shore. There was a place where hermit crabs by the hundreds scurried hither and yon into unoccupied holes in the inky-black sand. A pause in my walking connected me and grounded me in the *now* as my eyes took in the communal response of the crabs upon sensing my presence. The throng of busy hermit crabs safely in their sand bunkers was the signal for me to turn around and head back down the beach. As I turned around, I tried to catch a glimpse of the towering lifeguard stand in the village. It appeared miniaturized by the distance. I told myself, "You know you can do it"—i.e. walk to the village and turn once again to head back to #8. I felt triumphant and logged another day's mileage with satisfaction that I could taste on my salty lips.

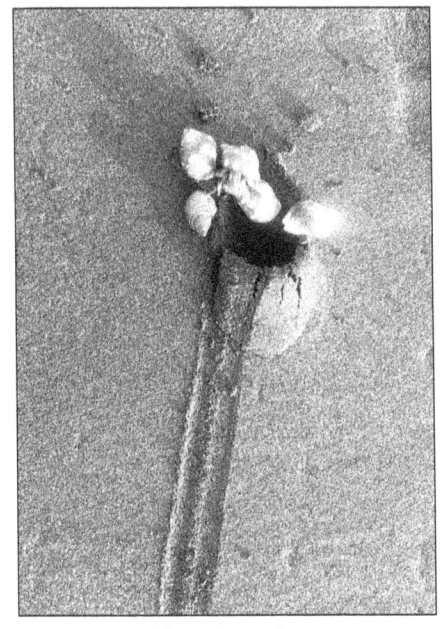

Hermit crabs

The Atlantic Ocean is only a six-hour drive from home, and the

South Carolina beaches along this shoreline have long since become our family gathering destination since before my birth. Over the years, we have gathered at the friendly, low-country beaches of Pawleys Island, DeBordieu, and Litchfield. My mother at 85-plus years still loved coming to the beach to spend precious time with her children, grandchildren, and great-grandchildren. In her later years, the car she traveled in was called the "Mimi mobile." When she arrived, it was like the Queen had arrived; everyone rushed out to see her and offered a hand in getting her safely inside, where children both young and old sat and talked, lingering with her as she enjoyed the rambling conversations. Everyone cherished the lazy days of summer beach week with her and each other.

Over the years, our numbers grew to more than 40. Litchfield Beach's accommodations met our need for varying sizes of lodging within walking distance of each other. Beach walking was a preferred means of visiting between condos and houses. For longer visits, cars were packed with beach chairs and gear as we made our way down the beach to be greeted by smiling faces and a hug-fest. Like my mother, I looked forward to long beach walks with my husband, children, and grandchildren, as well as my nieces and nephews. It was a time of settling into conversations that began with newsy-catching-up topics to some more serious aspects of life—hopes, dreams, intentions, and disappointments. Those walks, purposefully chosen, continued throughout the week and remain some of my most memorable walks.

One lazy day, I was beach walking with my very fit nephew and his wife. I always walked in the middle so I could hear both of them as we walked and talked. We became deeply engaged in our conversation, which bordered on being serious. We were so engrossed in sharing the story that we lost sight of what was happening behind us. We began to notice the wind picking up, sand stinging the back of our calves, and felt a light sprinkle. When we turned around, there was a huge bank of jet-black clouds, dumping buckets of rain, and flashing jagged bolts of lightning! We were very nervous! Having no shelter in sight, we ran; it seemed faster than any racehorse. I held on tightly to my nephew's arm, and we took off! I was winded, but my strong, healthy legs propelled me forward and eventually back to safety. I only needed to stop once to catch my breath—otherwise, I believed I could, and with the help of my athletic nephew and his wife, so I did! My year's mantra helped me to stay the course. It was quite a run; one I hope never to repeat!

Sunrise and sunset beach walks were magical. The beach itself was washed clean of footsteps and signs of humans. Walkers were pensive and mostly quiet. Fishermen dotted the coast waiting for their "catch of the day." One step at a time, I began to feel the morning's sleepiness leave my body, awakening the energy for a new day of possibilities: reading under the beach umbrella while digging my toes in the warm sand and sipping cool water from my insulated water bottle, playing bocce and scoring points for my teams, making sand castles with my grandsons, and having chats or longer conversations with my adult children who balance their lives with hard work, family time, and a myriad of other responsibilities and choice activities. The walks at sunset settled my soul as night arrived and brought a sense of peace at the end of the day. The beauty found in Earth's cycles and seasons brought contentment. Beach walking...oh, beach walking, I wish you were closer.

Chapter 5

Inclement Weather

Not every day was suitable for outdoor walking. On days of frigid temperatures and stormy weather, I sought a climate-controlled space in which to walk. The gym scene was not my cup of tea, nor was a treadmill in my husband's shop. It was a dilemma. Being the nature lover that I am, the idea of indoor walking seemed incongruent. Not ideal, but because it was convenient, climate-controlled, and available both early and late, I chose the mall. I am not comfortable walking in scrunched up crowds or where the noise level is deafening, but my alternatives were slim. I learned that "mall walkers" were allowed inside one hour prior to the stores and kiosks opening. The piped-in music was barely audible, and there were only a handful of walkers. That was an okay fit; quiet and few people.

So, I walked. In the mall. For three to four miles. About one hour. I finally got into a rhythm and a zone where I blocked most things out and simply walked. However, one thing that was difficult to ignore was the luscious aromas coming from the food court as they began preparations for lunch. I purposefully left my purse locked in the trunk of my car, so no matter how drawn I was to those yummy smells, I had no money. I didn't want those temptations to sabotage the benefits of my walking. Only one time did I intentionally bring a little cash in with me. A warm, original, hand-twisted, mouth-watering, giant pretzel was too enticing for my senses. I unapologetically gave in and thoroughly enjoyed every morsel!

Mall walking was not my first preference, but it provided a place to continue my *1,000-mile walking challenge and the promise I made to myself*. I was at *peace* with that as I kept walking, almost every day, one foot in front of the other.

Chapter 6

Intentions Beyond Myself

It was important to me that my 75th year's walking challenge reached beyond myself. I looked for an avenue that would touch a diverse population in a tangible way. I researched virtual races for charity and decided that was a meaningful way to go. Participating in virtual races was logistically easy to do. I searched the web looking under "Virtual Races/Run Events," and there were many from which to choose. Each had the same basic goal: to raise money for noteworthy charities and causes by encouraging people to get moving and make a difference at the same time, benefiting the walker/runner and the people helped by the charity. That was it!

How does it work? A virtual run is one that a person runs or walks from any location, at their own pace and on their chosen timetable, days or weeks, until the predetermined goal is reached. The fees and donations gathered for a particular race go to the chosen cause. The participant may choose to walk solo or be part of a team. During 2022, I chose to walk solo, because this challenge was very personal to me. Through my smartwatch, a running tabulation of my miles was recorded on the chosen race's website, where I'd receive daily updates on my progress. In addition, some sites sent virtual postcards online describing the educational aspects of the designated charity. All participants paid a race fee between $17-$27, which included a race bib prior to the race and a beautiful medal when the race was completed. Additional donations were welcomed, but not required. Virtual walks helped me to remain motivated and to stay the course of walking 1,000 miles by year's end.

I enjoyed the virtual messages of encouragement that were sent from the walk organizers: "Way to go today," "Your pace was spot on," and "Only ten more miles to go; you can do it!" I enjoyed, and took to heart, the health benefits of slowly but surely feeling stronger in mind and body. My stress levels decreased significantly, and I seemed to handle life, in general, more easily. I never thought about using alcohol. I had more resilience for the days' happenings. I enjoyed the accountability and looked forward to reviewing my stats. My walking times improved from 20-minute miles to 16-minute miles with very little breathiness. My legs had toned somewhat. That sweet tooth—well, it still enticed me—thus, I had only five pounds of actual weight loss. My daughter reminded me that muscle weighs more than fat. I liked being reminded of that! I enjoyed walking virtually knowing others were also walking for worthy charities. I never lost sight of my mantra, "She believed she could, so she did!" Walking became part of my daily routine, just like brushing my teeth.

This daily routine, however, was not a rigid one. I gave myself a rest day here and there. I had calculated how many miles per month

I needed to log and used that as my touchstone. I ordered a custom calendar with favorite pictures of my supportive family members smiling at me. Being a paper and pen-type person, I referenced my smart watch tabulations and posted my weekly mileage on Saturdays. That coincided with the smart watch's recordings and made my tabulations accurate. At the end of each month, I kept a running total. I was motivated by seeing the calendar hanging on the side of the refrigerator as I walked past it numerous times during the day. In 2023, I used the same calendar to record my miles. When I told my friends this, they chuckled and looked confused, saying, "But you'll be a day off." My reply was, "Oh, sure, I realize that, but I love this calendar. I'll adjust for that! It reminds me of those who encouraged me during my 75th birthday challenge!"

What gratitude I have for all my cheerleaders! I was committed to this goal and the promise I made to myself.

Chapter 7

My Virtual Walks

SHE BELIEVED SHE COULD, SO SHE DID

The first virtual race I participated in was "She Believed She Could, So She Did" and was sponsored by *Gone for a Run*. It was a marathon, 26.2 miles, and the charity was Americares. I felt this race was appropriate to begin my 1,000-mile challenge since it bore the name of my mantra and spoke to me with intention. Established in 1979, Americares saves lives and improves the health of people affected by poverty or disaster, enabling them to reach their full potential. Americares is one of the leading non-profit providers of medical aid to the US healthcare safety net, serving 1,000 clinics and more than 7 million patients in need. It has distributed $20 billion in humanitarian aid to 164 countries worldwide. Of the funds raised, 98% goes directly to global aid. Every $10 donation can provide $200 in aid. So, I walked...

Man's Best Friend

This walk was in honor of Molly, our 11-year-old Cavachon pup, who was a participant and the best motivator on many of my walks. I chose a 64.8-mile race, sponsored by *Yes Fit*, called "Man's Best Friend." The charity that benefited was the ASPCA. In 1866, Henry Bergh founded the ASPCA to provide an effective means for the prevention of cruelty to animals throughout the United States. According to Charity Navigator, the ASPCA has a rating of 83% direct aid. The scope of the ASPCA today has expanded to all of North America where it provides local and national leadership in animal-assisted therapy, animal behavior, animal poison control, anti-cruelty, humane education, legislative services, and shelter outreach. Molly's presence added sunshine and enthusiasm to my walking—truly "*Woman's Best Friend!*" So, I walked...

The Human Ear

Hearing is a part of the human experience and one that I took for granted, thinking I would always have it. That turned out not to be the case. As early as my mid-fifties, I began noticing I was missing parts of conversations with family and friends. I often misheard words, which led to misunderstandings. I loved to listen to singer-songwriters and their stories, but their lyrics were escaping me. TV Ears and closed captioning were the only ways I could access TV. I could not hear my own voice. The quality of my life was diminishing. It became increasingly more difficult, until I *finally* admitted to myself and my family, especially my daughter, who is a Doctor of Audiology, that I needed help. After years of urging me to have my hearing checked, I agreed. The hearing care provided by my daughter and her colleagues has been life changing. With hearing aids, the quality of my interactions with others has been enhanced greatly. Listening to music and fully grasping the lyrics puts a smile on my face, and bird songs thrill me again, whether I am in my own backyard or walking and hiking the trails. Once again, I participated fully with my family, making memories with those I love. All in all, I became acutely aware of the richness of life all around me...every day. What a gift!

To honor my daughter and her colleagues in their compassionate work to provide hearing solutions to those who have never heard before and to restore the hearing of those whose hearing has significantly diminished or faded entirely, I chose a virtual run marathon entitled "The Human Ear." This walk was sponsored by *Moon Joggers* and benefited The Starkey Hearing Foundation, whose mission is to give the gift of hearing to those in need, empowering them to achieve their potential.

As a young man, William F. Austin realized his life's purpose, and that simply was to help people hear. After years of laying out his vision to bring his efforts to fruition, William and his wife, Tani, co-founded the Starkey Hearing Foundation in 1984. Their premise was, "Alone, we can't do much. Together, we can change the world." Together they moved tirelessly toward creating sustainable, community-based hearing healthcare solutions. In structuring the Starkey Foundation, they set up two Core Pillars. One pillar is Education and Capacity Building. The second is Global Advocacy.

As a part of the Education and Capacity Building pillar, they established the first Starkey Hearing Institute in Lusaka, Zambia. The purpose was to address the dire shortage of hearing healthcare professionals in Africa. Graduates of the institute returned to their native countries as hearing healthcare champions. They made an immediate impact by organizing care centers in their own communities.

As a part of the Global Advocacy pillar, the Foundation has delivered care through international missions to over 100 countries around the world, including the United States. Over 200,000 free hearing aids have been fitted globally each year. HEAR NOW is a domestic program of the Starkey Hearing Foundation that provides hearing aids to people in the United States with no other resources with which to acquire hearing aids. As the only completely American-owned and operated provider of hearing solutions, Starkey is proud to support our veterans.

The Starkey Hearing Foundation believes that "life is made up of sharing ideas, dreams, and goals. Hearing is vital to that. Giving one person the gift of hearing may seem like a small act of kindness, but it has a compounding effect on the future of the world."

This charity touched me deeply and personally. So, I walked...

Run For Peace/Stand With Ukraine

During 2022, the war in Ukraine escalated, and the United States and other allies began supporting the Ukrainians with their fight to preserve their democracy. Volodymyr Zelenskyy has been the Head of State in Ukraine since 2019 and continues to courageously fight the Russian army as it bombards their cities and innocent civilians. I often feel helpless to *do* anything to help in relief efforts. I searched for a charitable run and found one named "Run for Peace/Stand with Ukraine," sponsored by *E-Runner*. The charity, Ukraine Relief, united athletes in the Biggest Peace Virtual Marathon ever. It seems like such a small part, but unifying for peace may help save one life. So, I walked...

Mount Everest

Walking 1,000 miles or climbing 40 miles to the summit of Mount Everest are both commendable achievements. However, the 40 mile-summit of Mount Everest is Earth's highest mountain. It reaches an elevation of 29,029 feet above sea level. The *Conqueror Challenge* sponsored a race called "Mount Everest." It was a 40-mile walk, and the charity was Plastic Bank. Plastic Bank was founded in 2013 by David Katz and Shawn Frankson. According to plasticbank.com, its mission is to stop plastic bottles *before* they enter the ocean.

The plastic bottles collected are delivered to processing partners

Virtual postcard from "Mount Everest" race.

for reprocessing into feedstock, which is reused in manufacturing products and packaging by the world's most progressive companies. Plastic Bank has stopped 16,476,450 plastic bottles to date from entering the ocean. As I walked these 40 miles in 14 days, I became keenly aware of my own plastic footprint and pledged to do what I could to reduce my use of plastic bottles. During my walks along the shores of the glistening waters of the Atlantic and Pacific Oceans, I felt an urgency—both in disseminating information to others and being an example for others to become stewards of our oceans. So, I walked...

FLIGHT OF THE MONARCH BUTTERFLY

My love of nature and commitment to monarch butterfly education inspired me to choose a race entitled "Flight of the Monarch Butterfly," which was sponsored by *Yes.Fit*. It was a 100-mile walking challenge for me and a 2,500-mile flight challenge for my partner, the monarch butterfly. What is meant by partnering with a butterfly? This is the scenario: the monarch's starting point was in Mastigouche Wildlife Reserve, Quebec, Canada. Its finish was in the Monarch Butterfly Biosphere Reserve high in the Sierra Madre Mountains, Michoacán, Mexico. For every mile I walked, the online monarch butterfly "flew" 25 miles.

I completed this challenge in 24 days. The monarch takes about two months to complete its 2,500-mile challenge. *Yes.Fit* sent daily map updates on the monarch's progress in relation to the number

> "The question is not merely to survive, but to thrive; and to do so with passion, compassion, humor, and style."
> — Maya Angelou

of miles I had walked. It was very motivating to check my stats at the end of the day and see exactly where in Canada, the United States, or Mexico my monarch partner was roosting that night! The funds raised during this race went directly into Monarch education and preservation. So, I walked...

THE SAGA OF THE MONARCH BUTTERFLY

The monarch butterfly is one of the most amazing creatures on our planet! This insect's resilience in surviving a 2,500-mile fall/spring migration from Canada through the United States arriving in Mexico with perfect timing is astonishing. The spring migration from Mexico to Canada is equally astonishing!

Journey North is an organization that began in 1994 with founder Elizabeth Howard's vision of combining the emerging technology of the internet and the interconnectedness of all things. Today's climate crisis, the use of herbicides and pesticides, and habitat loss threaten many migratory species, including the monarch butterfly. The number of these iconic butterflies has plummeted by 80% in the last 20 years according to the Center for Biological Diversity. In July of 2022, the International Union for Conservation of Nature (IUCN) reclassified the migratory monarch butterfly as endangered on its "red list."

In 2008, prior to the Monarch's being listed on the endangered list, my husband and I, along with four friends, joined a group of educators in Atlanta called Monarchs Across Georgia and traveled to the Monarch overwintering sanctuaries of El Rosario, El Capulan on Pelon Massif, and Sierra Chincua. These areas are sites where the monarchs spend their winters roosting in oyamel fir trees. Enormous clusters of monarchs hang in the trees in a semi-hibernating state, only leaving the clusters on sunny days to sip water from the nearby streams. As a group, we wanted to experience this amazing phenomenon as eyewitnesses. What we did not fully comprehend was that the terrain over which we would travel was neither a direct path nor easy. The remote locations were at 10,000 feet elevation. Hiking that trek was impossible. It was one of those times when one's curiosity was piqued, but answers to questions dribbled in.

From our arrival at the airport in Mexico City, we traveled by bus to the friendly town of Angangueo, Michoacán. The town was tucked into the mountains, and the people warmly welcomed visitors who were there to see the butterflies. Many in the surrounding little towns depended on tourism as their only source of income. Don Bruno, our modest hotel, was comfortable and served delicious, authentic Mexican food. After a restful night's sleep and hearty breakfast, we were surprised to see a rickety, wood-sided, blue pick-up truck waiting for us outside the hotel. With happy hearts and crossed fingers, we used cautious movements to climb into the truck bed. Some were sitting, and others were standing. As the truck started up the steep rocky road, we held on for dear life!

We pulled our bandanas up to cover our noses and mouths as clouds of brown dust kicked up in our faces with every turn of the tires. Every time the driver shifted into a lower gear, he crossed himself! The racket from the crankshaft was heart-stopping. Despite all the noise, rocky terrain, and nerve-racking commotion, we traveled up the mountain until we could go no farther. We had arrived at the Monarch Butterfly Biosphere Reserve. We steadied ourselves as we climbed down from the old, dilapidated truck. We explored the area a bit before settling into an open-air cabana where delicious Mexican tacos were being prepared right before our eyes. Oh, the savory aromas and mouthwatering tastes fortified us in a most pleasing way as we prepared for the afternoon adventure. We forged ahead.

Next, we traveled by horse. Each horse was specifically chosen for its rider and led by a caballero. We made our way through the thicketed and rocky paths until the horses could go no farther... about an hour's ride. Dismounting from our horses, we thanked our guides and began to walk the remainder of the rugged trail, one foot in front of the other for another hour. We arrived at a place 10,000 feet in elevation, where millions of monarchs were roosting in the oyamel fir trees. The sun brilliantly shone on these beautiful insects.

The dreams I had dreamt, the books I had read, the route I had traveled by airplane, bus, rickety truck, horse, and on foot—none of this came close to preparing me for what was revealed to me through my eyes and ears. As I approached the massive clusters of roosting monarchs, my eyes wide open, I was captivated by the wonderment of it all. There was a sense of reverence among others around us as a collective hush fell over the group. I visually drank in the beauty around me. I was mesmerized when I realized I could hear the gently flapping wings of the monarchs as they left the clusters to bask in the sun and sip from the cool streams and puddles. I was awestruck! The group lingered there for quite a while, sitting on rocks, leaning against trees, moving slowly and quietly for another view—all eyes gazing upward and beyond. These images are engraved in my consciousness, never to be forgotten. As the time arrived for us to leave this spellbinding place, I could feel a gentle nudge and hear a little voice whispering, "Do more," and to share this experience with others.

For over a decade following this experience, I felt compelled, and happily so, to share with others the amazing life of the monarch butterfly. Sharing is caring, and this amazing insect's phenomenal life and migration are worth it!

The settings for the educational endeavors included elementary schools, garden clubs, local nature groups, nursing homes, church events, and neighborhood children. I prepared PowerPoint presentations for each group that were specifically designed for that age and/or interest group. In addition, I brought live monarchs in all four stages of the life cycle. I used two aquariums: one for eggs and small caterpillars, and one for medium to adult caterpillars. When the adult caterpillars were ready to pupate, they formed in the top portion of the aquarium. I used a tall, netted enclosure for live monarch butterflies, which we would release after the presentation.

The wonder and awe on the faces of participants, ranging from 3 to 80+ years old, made me smile. All who were present, when a chrysalis formed or the moment a butterfly pushed through the chrysalis revealing a newly enclosed butterfly, were fascinated by

> **Meet your neighbors**
> An occasional look at interesting people in Upper East Tennessee

Aubrie Abernethy has incorporated teaching into her life since she was a small child, and her style continues to lean away from the traditional stand-at-the-blackboard-and-instruct mode toward a freer, more exploratory method that helps students weave together basic learning skills.

The skillful thinker is now a private tutor who uses unique techniques to engage students' senses in ways that help them understand math, reading and science. She also has incorporated an extensive knowl-

puzzles and other hands-on tools to engage the young to the elderly.

"My mother and daddy gave me a hallway closet when I was just a young kid," she said while surrounded by a stock of her offbeat but clever teaching tools. "That was my first school. I wrote little math problems and stories. I was playing school, and my stuffed

▶ See **WING**, Page 10A

Aubrie Abernethy has incorporated an extensive knowledge of Monarch butterflies and employs everything from eggs, larvae, a working set of wings, puzzles and other hands-on tools in her teaching to engage the young to the elderly.

Newspaper article in *Johnson City Press.*

what they saw. Every experience was unique in its details, but the thread that tied all these experiences together was the heightening of the wonder and curiosity urging all of us *to do* something, ever so small. *Do something* to help preserve the amazing monarch butterfly. Plant milkweeds. Plant native flowers as nectar sources. Use only insecticidal soap for pests. It does not harm the caterpillars.

Embrace dandelions, clover, and wild violets in your yard as food for rabbits and other small visitors, and as nectar sources for our winged friends, including pollinators that breeze by. Read books, educate yourself, and tell others. It's the small actions that make the biggest difference. *Do something...*

My enthusiasm for the preservation of the monarch butterfly provided the impetus for me to add "The Flight of the Monarch" virtual race to my walking challenge. By doing so, I hope I helped to educate the next generation about the perilous time for this amazing insect and how individuals can get involved. Together, let's *walk the talk!*

Coram

As my year of intentional walking progressed, I continued to be motivated by participating in virtual races for charity. During 2022, Great Britain experienced great joy and deep sadness. Great joy in honoring Queen Elizabeth II as the longest-serving monarch in British history—a remarkable 70 years, and deep mourning for her sudden death at age 96. Well into her nineties, Queen Elizabeth remained faithful in maintaining hundreds of charitable organizations and programs, one of which was Coram. I chose two races supporting Coram. "The Queen's Platinum Jubilee 2022" was sponsored by *Medal Mad*. "God Saved the Queen April 21, 1926–September 8, 2022" was sponsored by *Virtual Run Events*.

Coram, the world's first children's charity, was established by

Royal Charter in 1739. This charity continues to help more than one million children, young people, and their families every year. Today's Coram is a thriving group of specialist organizations working in the UK and around the world. Among these organizations is one which finds adoptive and foster homes for vulnerable children and offers support to their families. Coram Voice champions the rights of children in their care, making sure that they know their rights and can navigate the system. Coram Youth Projects places young people in roles within the Coram organization. Coram's Support Gateway provides parents with the support and advice they may need at all stages of parenthood. Coram's Creative Therapies team offers art and music services to children, youth, and their families. Many other Coram-sponsored educational and legal organizations supporting the children, youth, and their families are in place to improve their lives long term.

Coram's approach is to listen, innovate, advocate, and support, in order to achieve long-lasting changes for children and their families worldwide. This mission touched me deeply. So, I walked...

Operation Warm

As a young child, it never occurred to me that there were children without warm coats and sturdy shoes. It was not until my world as a child expanded that I came to realize having a warm winter coat and comfortable shoes to wear is a privilege not every child enjoys.

The virtual race named "Believe in the Magic" was a marathon sponsored by *Virtual Run Events*. The charity this race supported was Operation Warm. Operation Warm is a national, nonprofit organization that manufactures brand-new, high-quality coats and shoes for children in need. During its 24-year history, Operation Warm has served over 5,000,000 children in over 2,100 communities. Operation Warm brings hope not only by providing those basic needs and physical warmth, but also emotional warmth which fosters self-confidence and hope for a brighter future. Providing coats and shoes to children was a responsibility close to my heart. As an elementary school teacher in a school where children in my classroom often needed warm coats and shoes, I felt a deep connection. A child who comes to school cold starts her day at a disadvantage. Meeting these needs changes a child's perspective and sets the stage for better learning. Self-confidence and smiles radiate from children's faces when they are empowered by such simple necessities in life. So, I walked...

BE BRAVE

All of us experience growing pains, no matter our age. My 10-year-old grandson and I shared a period of growth at the same time—both searching for peace from anxiety. While at "Camp Gigi," our special week-long time together two or three times each year, we decided to walk and talk with our intention being to help others, while we helped alleviate our anxious feelings.

The virtual race named "Be Brave" was the one we chose. It was sponsored by *Virtual Race Events and Moon Joggers*. The inspiration for this race came from the author A.A. Milne, as he wrote, "You're braver than you believe, stronger than you seem, and smarter than you think." This mantra spoke to both of us.

The charity this race supported was Be the Match, also known as NMDP (National Marrow Donor Program). The goal is to save lives through cell therapy. Find cures. Save lives. This global nonprofit leader in cell therapy was founded in 1981 by Amy Ronneberg with the purpose of matching patients to life-saving marrow transplants, cover uninsured costs for transplant recipients, and fund extensive research. This program has touched over 41 million potential donors, registered 811,000 blood units and facilitated 120,000 transplants since 1987. Being "brave" takes on an even greater meaning when you think of the lives of the recipients, whose lives have been saved, and the challenges they faced through this life-saving process and beyond. In addition, my grandson and I have grown stronger and much healthier, both in mind and body, as we strive to be brave when things get tough! So, we walked…

Happy Birthday to Me

One of the first nursery rhymes a child learns is "Twinkle Twinkle Little Star," where making a wish upon a star enchants the dreams of little dreamers.

The race that called to me was "Happy Birthday to Me 2022." It was a marathon sponsored by *Virtual Run Events* whose charity was the Make-a-Wish Foundation. My 75th birthday wish paled in comparison with the tens of thousands of life-changing wishes being granted to children with critical illnesses. For Wish kids, just formulating a wish can give them the courage to comply with the medical treatments they need. Making a wish helps children believe anything is possible. Wishes also support families of these children as they overcome anxiety and reach out to other families. Since 1980, the Make-a-Wish Foundation has remained steadfast in its mission to work together to bring hope and transformation to seriously ill children by granting their wishes. A wish is granted every 34 minutes. With the help of 32,000 volunteers worldwide, Make-a-Wish has collectively granted more than 520,000 wishes, making it the world's largest wish-granting organization.

From the twinkling little star to the Make-a-Wish Foundation, wishes really do come true.

The charity virtual races discussed in this memoir are but a few of the causes I supported while walking 1,000 miles. There were actually 30 virtual races I participated in during this time. Each one felt like I was connected to a force bigger than myself. I hope my small part made a difference for those who needed help to become their best selves. In helping them, my life was enriched beyond measure. So, I walked...

Chapter 8

Reflections

During the year, my emotional state remained upbeat and positive for the most part. From time to time, I took short breaks of a day or two, but soon I felt ready to continue walking, because the walking itself was mentally energizing as the endorphins flowed through my body. Psychologically, I felt gratified that I was being true to my intention of walking 1,000 miles as I sought a healthier life ahead, spending quality time with my family and friends. I honestly did not feel discouraged during my challenge. On the contrary, the feelings of improved health and peace within were motivators in themselves, as I remembered the promise I made to myself. I believed I could, and I did! My 1,000th mile was walked on December 21, 2022, the Winter Solstice.

I chose this day specifically. I felt that concluding this personal challenge on the solstice revealed a metaphorical truth. This truth is beautifully expressed in a poem by Stephanie Laird, who was inspired by Native American thought.

The Winter Solstice Blessing

"May you find peace in the promise of the solstice night
That each day forward is blessed with more light.
That cycle of nature, unbroken and true,
Brings faith to your soul and well-being to you.
Rejoice in the darkness, in silence find rest,
And may the days that follow be absolutely blessed."

I had reached my goal of walking 1,000 miles, one step at a time, day in and day out, inside and outside. On the Winter Solstice, I took time to reflect in the darkness, rest, and look forward to the coming light, and yet another year to continue...walking. I had found *peace in the promise that I made to myself.*

Epilogue

After successfully completing my walking challenge, I asked a friend to help me make a map in order to visualize 1,000 miles. With his help and mapdevelopers.com, I drew a circle with a radius stretching 1,000 miles where HOME, Johnson City, TN, was the circle's center. I was astonished at the geographic locations that lay on the points generally north, south, east, and west, 1,000 miles from HOME.

I printed the maps in a series of different prospectives, zooming out each time. The series included three photos: half of the United States, the Western Hemisphere, and the entire world. When I looked at these images, it was a jaw-dropping experience. This 1,000-mile radius from HOME outward in all directions stunned my eyes and excited my imagination! I was energized after completing this memoir! My love for historical fiction cranked into gear. Should I write a Part 2 as historical fiction? I began to outline the plot and create characters, deciding what could happen on the adventures to the north in Quebec, Canada; to the east in the Bermuda Triangle; to the south in Cuba; and to the west in the heartland of Oklahoma.

Oh, the places I could go, and the people I could meet! But that story will have to wait for another time...

My 75th Year's 1,000 Mile Walking Challenge

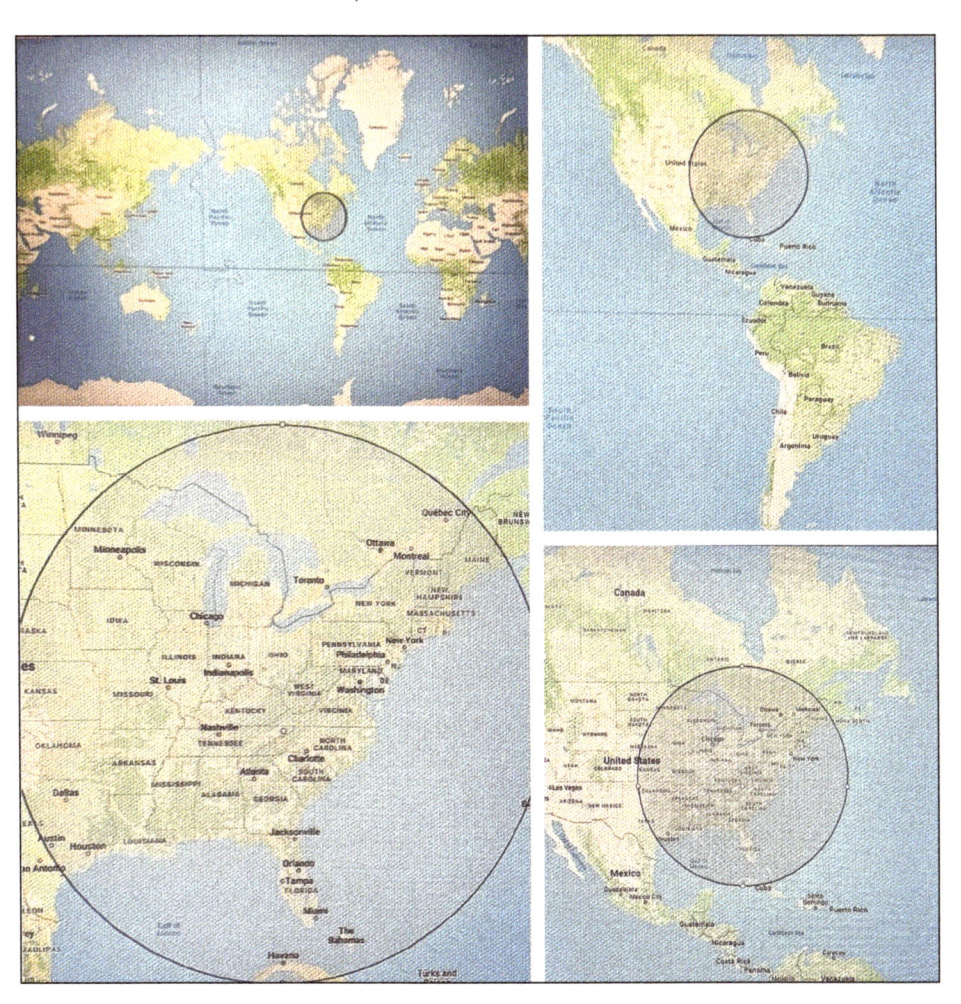

With Gratitude

The year of walking 1,000 miles and a second year for writing this memoir were two of the most focused years of my life. When one is keenly focused on a goal(s), oftentimes their world shrinks a bit for other activities of daily life.

First and foremost, I want to lovingly thank my husband, Jim, who became my "soul" supporter, encouraging me to stay strong. His warm smile and huge hug prior to my walking spurred me on. His patience for simplifying homelife cleared a space in my Type-A brain so that I could walk, nap, or write. For that and so much more, I am deeply grateful. Jim, you are my rock!

To all my wonderful and supportive family and friends who were steadfast in keeping up with my progress and cheering me on, rain or shine—thank you for your heartfelt cheerleading!

To my dear friends, Nancy Barrigar and Pam Blair, thank you for sharing your literary expertise in helping to edit this memoir. Your support during the process kept me on track as the manuscript became a reality. Your listening ears and scholarly edits guided me to publication. Thank you for walking with me vicariously!

To Janie Jessee and Jan-Carol Publishing, Inc. team for their advice and support during the editing and design phases of this book. Your professionalism helped to bring my story to life!

About the Author

Aubrie Abernethy was born in Johnson City, Tennessee, where she lives with her husband, Jim, and their dog, Molly. She received a BA degree from Converse College and a MAT degree from East Tennessee State University. She taught elementary school children during her career as a teacher, and after her retirement, tutored children in her home. She has always enjoyed personal journaling and writing descriptive narratives. During her college days, she wrote poetry. Throughout her life, she has felt a deep connection to the natural world. The experiences of hiking, walking, and observing brought her much joy. This book, her first, was written to share insights she had as she intentionally walked 1,000 miles during the year she turned 75 years old.

7/25